MW00656907

Life Begins at the
End of Your Comfort Zone

Life Begins at the End of Your Comfort Zone

Reignite · Renew · Refuel

A JOURNAL

Jacqueline Lewis

ROCK
POINT

How to Use This Journal

YOU DON'T HAVE TO READ THIS JOURNAL IN ONE FELL SWOOP.

You definitely shouldn't try to rush through the exercises. Feel free to dip in and out. Scan the sections. Do the exercises that jump out at you. Maybe a different section will resonate with you on another day.

It's all right if you don't do every prompt. It's also okay if you don't finish the exercises, or even this book. Some folks might want to take a week's retreat and focus intensively on the journal. Some may buy copies for friends for a girls' weekend away. Others may labor in solitude over the course of a year, or two, growing incrementally. There's no wrong way to use this journal.

CONTENTS

What Gets Measured Gets Done

The basic premise behind this journal is this: what gets measured gets done. This journal gives you a place to hold yourself accountable, to measure your progress and record your victories. It's a guide from where you are now to where you want to be. It may not always be easy or comfortable, but we promise it will be stimulating, useful, and fun.

Each section is followed by exercises or writing prompts to help you delve more fully into the topic. Feel free to adapt the exercises any way you'd like. When it comes to this project, it's all about you.

SEVEN
Things You Need to Know

This journal is built around seven core ideas. Master any one of them and you will feel better and stronger. Master all seven and you will be noticeably happier and braver. Other people will be drawn to your calm, confidence, and joy.

THESE SEVEN THINGS WE KNOW TO BE TRUE:

1. You're okay just as you are.

2. Lead with your strengths.

3. Adding is more fun than subtracting.

4. Things will work out—they always do.

5. Find the fun.

6. See the good.

7. The stories we tell create the people we become.

Getting out of your

COMFORT ZONE

Rule #1

You're Okay Just as You Are

Reignite Your Life

Ever spend time with a toddler? They are never bored. Three-year-olds move, climb, clamber; they explore, and ignore, boundaries. They fall a lot, too. Can you recapture that boundless enthusiasm? Harness the foolhardy fearlessness of a young child? Yes, you can. You have all the tools you need to reignite your life, right within these pages. Let's get started.

So you've just opened a journal designed to launch you out of your comfort zone. And the very first thing we have to tell you is this: you're okay just as you are.

Photographer JJ Tizou noticed that many of his subjects felt uncomfortable and self-critical in front of the camera. In response, he wrote a manifesto called "Everyone Is Photogenic" (www.everyoneisphotogenic. com), proclaiming, "People are beautiful when they're finding joy in life, being kind to others, and enjoying themselves." Wise words. Many of us are our own worst critics. No one is perfect. Before you move beyond your comfort zone, it's first key to trust that you are okay just the way you are.

If only we gave ourselves the same compassion and empathy we lavish on others!

Stop "Mean-Girling" Yourself

The 2004 film *Mean Girls* captures the casual cruelty teens lob at each other. But sometimes we are our own worst enemies. Do you carry around an internalized "mean girl," chiding yourself for your shortcomings? Let's silence that critical voice (after we take a minute to hear what it has to say). This journal is no place to lament past decisions or stew in regret. Sure, we all make mistakes. Mine are legion. But those mistakes are in the past. They have little to do with our work here in the present.

We can't undo our mistakes; we can just try not to repeat them. Obsessing over things we wish we'd done differently saps energy that we need in order to live well now. It can lead to depression. Worrying about what comes next also saps our energy. This book occupies the space between the flawed past and the unknown future—the present. The present is a place of possibility and equilibrium. This journal will ask you to peek into your past or peer into the future. But the work will be done in the here and now. Now is all we have.

Remember, you are okay just the way you are. Stop finding fault with yourself. It's time to shift the focus to the many things you've gotten right.

Meet Your Bodacious Self

Moving outside your comfort zone will require bravery and self-knowledge. You need to know who you are now in order to figure out who you want to be. Are you taking yourself for granted? When was the last time you sat down and thought about what makes you tick?

Let's first jump ahead to the final day of your life. Think about that common question: "If you knew you were going to die tomorrow, how would you spend your last day?" No need to be morbid about it. Sit back and think: how would you design the perfect day? If you had sufficient resources, where would you wake up? Would you be alone, or with someone? Would you linger in bed, or get moving? What meals would you eat? Would you remain frenetically busy, packing in as much as possible, or would you seek solitude and relaxation? Would you seek out experiences you hadn't yet had? Places you'd not yet seen? Or bask in the familiar; doing the things you love most one last time?

Describe your perfect day.
Write down every last detail you can think of.

======

....

....

....

....

....

....

....

....

....

....

....

....

....

....

Describe your perfect day.
Write down every last detail you can think of.
(continued)

....

....

....

....

....

....

....

....

....

....

....

....

....

Describe your perfect day.
Write down every last detail you can think of.

(continued)

. . . .

. . . .

. . . .

. . . .

. . . .

. . . .

. . . .

. . . .

. . . .

. . . .

. . . .

. . . .

. . . .

Describe your perfect day.
Write down every last detail you can think of.
(continued)

....
....
....
....
....
....
....
....
....
....
....
....
....
....

Describe your perfect day.
Write down every last detail you can think of.
(continued)

....
....
....
....
....
....
....
....
....
....
....
....
....

How does this ultimate day compare to your everyday life? What are the similarities?

========

What are the differences?

Whom do you admire? Why?

....
....
....
....
....
....
....
....
....
....
....
....
....
....
....
....
....

What's your favorite quality about yourself?

....

....

....

....

....

....

....

....

....

....

....

....

....

....

....

How is your life different than you imagined it would be?

....

....

....

....

....

....

....

....

....

....

....

....

....

....

Who are you genuinely happy to see?
Why?

....
....
....
....
....
....
....
....
....
....
....
....
....
....
....

Who is happiest to see you?
What do they see in you?

....

....

....

....

....

....

....

....

....

....

....

....

....

What would you do with your time if you didn't have to earn a living?

....

....

....

....

....

....

....

....

....

....

....

....

....

How can you incorporate aspects of your ideal day into your every day?

....

....

....

....

....

....

....

....

....

....

....

....

....

Getting out of your

COMFORT ZONE

Rule #2

Lead with Your Strengths

Lead with Your Strengths

When we seek change, it's tempting to focus on what's "wrong" or lacking. Any meaningful change, however, will come from strengths you already have, skills you've already mastered. You can't lead from the broken places.

Psychologist Martin Seligman shifted the course of modern psychology with a simple decision to study human success rather than pathology. Take some time to focus on your strengths. As Winnie the Pooh says, you are stronger than you seem.

Recall a time when you felt strong and confident.

....

....

....

....

....

....

....

....

....

....

....

....

....

....

....

What have you accomplished that you set out to do?

....
....
....
....
....
....
....
....
....
....
....
....
....
....
....

If you were a superhero what superpower would you want to have. And why?

....

....

....

....

....

....

....

....

....

....

....

....

....

....

Getting out of your

COMFORT ZONE

Rule #3

Adding Is More Fun Than Subtracting

Have you ever dieted? Fads come and go, but nearly every popular trend tells us what to avoid. No fat. No sugar. No gluten. No meat. These models of deprivation may work in the short run, but who can sustain a lifetime of resistance? Who would want to? The most sustainable, authentic change comes from embracing abundance, the notion that the world is filled with good things and there is enough for everybody.

From a healthy eating perspective, this means adding wonderful things to your diet and your day. Fresh fruits and vegetables. Red wine. Physical activities you enjoy. Focus on what you can have, what you can do. Before you know it, the healthy choices have crowded out the less healthy ones. This doesn't mean you have to stop eating ice cream for breakfast. Really! If that's your thing, have at it. But if the rest of your day is filled with yoga and healthy meals, it will all balance out.

This approach extends past diet and exercise. Keep adding positive changes to your day and inevitably those choices will crowd out those less-ideal habits you'd love to shake.

What healthy decision can you add to your day?

....

....

....

....

....

....

....

....

....

....

....

....

....

Put on Your Own Oxygen Mask before Assisting Others

You can't drive a car without gas and you can't ride a horse without feeding him hay. Yet many of us blaze through life running on empty, not taking the time to fuel ourselves properly, either physically or mentally.

The following four aspects of our lives affect nearly every bit of our happiness and health. Lucky for us, most of them can be controlled.

1. How much we move

2. What we eat and drink

3. The space around us

4. Whom we choose to spend time with

Move What You've GOT!

When it comes to our bodies and mobility, it's use it or lose it. Staying active doesn't just make us strong and fit; it literally keeps our cells supple and our mood positive. Seek easy ways to incorporate movement into your daily life. You might park at the far end of the parking lot. Bike to work. Take a walk after dinner. Use small weights at home or at work. Take the stairs instead of the elevator. Remember, what gets measured gets done.

List the ways you can increase your physical activity. What new skill or sport would you like to explore? List two, along with a concrete step to take (e.g., sign up for lessons, buy equipment).

....

....

....

....

....

....

You Are What You Eat (and Drink)

We've all felt it. Suddenly out of nowhere, your body is dragging. You realize your head is pounding. Stiff and icky, foggy and achy, your body is just not where it needs to be. Sometimes the answer is as simple as dehydration, hidden hunger, or too little sleep. There is a direct connection between how we take care of ourselves and how we feel.

How much sleep do you need? What changes can you make to your diet to help you feel stronger and healthier?

....

....

....

....

....

....

....

....

What new skills do you want to learn?

1. ....
2. ....
3. ....
4. ....
5. ....
6. ....
7. ....
8. ....
9. ....
10. ....
11. ....
12. ....
13. ....
14. ....
15. ....

Make a plan for how you are going to accomplish learning these new skills.

=====

....

....

....

....

....

....

....

....

....

....

....

....

....

Getting out of your

COMFORT ZONE

Rule #4

Things Will Work Out— They Always Do

n 1923, economist John Maynard Keynes said, "In the long run we are all dead." Worrying about what comes next saps our energy. The things we worry about most rarely come to pass, while the most awful, life-changing telephone calls usually appear out of thin air. Anxiety and worry are emotions of the future, a future over which we have little control.

The Persian poet Attar of Nishapur is credited with a fable about a king who sought a device to make him happy when he was sad. His counselors presented him with a ring inscribed with the words "This too shall pass." The world is ephemeral. Change is the only constant. Cultivate the conviction that things will work out, one way or another. It might not be the outcome you sought, but you will get through it.

We do all sorts of things every day that once seemed impossibly difficult. If we only did what we were good at, we'd all still be crawling instead of walking.

Recall a time when you felt lost or frustrated. How did you turn it around?

....

....

....

....

....

....

....

....

....

....

....

....

....

....

....

....

List some difficult things you have endured.

1. ....
2. ....
3. ....
4. ....
5. ....
6. ....
7. ....
8. ....
9. ....
10. ....

How were you able to get through them?

....

....

....

....

....

....

....

....

....

....

....

....

....

....

....

Getting out of your

COMFORT ZONE

Rule #5

Find the Fun

Are you having enough fun? It's easy to succumb to the relentless cycle of work, home, errands, bills, obligations. Many of us limp along, busy, sleep-deprived, and waiting for our "real" lives to begin. It needn't be that way. There is fun, mischief, and whimsy to be had every day, if we just make room for it. Resolve to find the fun as habitually as you take a daily vitamin or drink your morning coffee. Your life will instantly become more, well, fun. Folks will start gravitating toward you.

Whimsy is underrated. As children, we play naturally, joyfully, inventively using the materials at hand. Why should that have to stop?

What was your favorite toy as a child? Why?

What was your favorite game as a child? Why?

....

....

....

....

....

....

....

....

....

....

....

....

....

....

List fifteen things you have done recently that were fun.

1. ....
2. ....
3. ....
4. ....
5. ....
6. ....
7. ....
8. ....
9. ....
10. ....
11. ....
12. ....
13. ....
14. ....
15. ....

Try to incorporate the things you love to do for fun into your daily life. Make a plan and write it down.

Make a Happy and Joyful Playlist.

1. ....
2. ....
3. ....
4. ....
5. ....
6. ....
7. ....
8. ....
9. ....
10. ....
11. ....
12. ....
13. ....
14. ....
15. ....

What songs make you feel most connected to yourself?

1. ....
2. ....
3. ....
4. ....
5. ....
6. ....
7. ....
8. ....
9. ....
10. ....
11. ....
12. ....
13. ....
14. ....
15. ....

Creative
SPARK

J ulia Cameron, author of the groundbreaking book on creativity, *The Artist's Way*, says, "The creative process is a process of surrender, not control." Too often we think we need to direct our creative impulse, when in fact the creative impulse directs us. That is how all art is made.

You can't spell sparkle without S-P-A-R-K. Coloring or drawing connects us with our most authentic self. There are no words to get in the way. Use the coloring and drawing pages here take a deep breath and see where your hands take you. They are perfect for quieting the judgmental voice in your head and letting your creative self take over.

Draw & Sketch

Draw & Sketch

Draw & Sketch

Getting out of your

COMFORT ZONE

Rule #6

See the Good

The world is filled with wonderful things just waiting to be noticed, many of them right under our very noses. We can find what we're looking for, so let's keep our eyes on all that's good and beautiful and possible in the world. How can you find the good in your life every day? Write about the ways that you can always find the good in your life no matter what life throws at you.

=================

....

....

....

....

....

....

....

Gratitude is a state of mind that makes you richer without adding a penny to your pocket. It bolsters your immune system and improves your mental outlook. It makes problems appear more manageable.

———————————

Being grateful begins with a focus on what we have right this minute: small things that are easy to overlook, large things that maybe we take for granted.

To lighten your load and get the full health benefits of gratitude, commit to a daily gratitude practice. All you need to do is notice and record five small items each day. Think about them as you are on your way to work or while you are waiting in line at the store. The very act of identifying things to appreciate will make you more aware and more grateful. Gratitude is a habit.

List five specific things you are grateful for:

1. ....

....

2. ....

....

3. ....

....

4. ....

....

5. ....

....

Getting out of your

COMFORT ZONE

Rule #7

The Stories We Tell Create the People We Become

"For there is nothing either good
or bad, but thinking makes it so."

HAMLET, ACT 2, SCENE 2, LINES 239–251

If you take away just one piece of wisdom from this
book, let it be this: The stories we tell create the people
we become. The power of narrative—telling the same
story a different way—can reshape our lives without
changing one thing about it.

What story do you tell yourself about your life, and how can you tell a better one?

======

....
....
....
....
....
....
....
....
....
....
....
....
....
....
....
....

Knowing What to Do Is the Easy Part

There are many reasons people fear change. Our comfort zone is, well, comfortable. It's what we know. It's worked for us so far. Or it hasn't. But it's a known quantity compared to what else might be out there.

Fear of the Unknown

Fear of the unknown could be due to lack of preparation. Maybe it's not that we don't want change, we just don't feel ready for it. What if we don't have the skills to tackle the new reality? What if it comes too fast? What might happen as you move beyond your comfort zone?

What roadblocks are preventing you from achieving your goals?

....

....

....

....

....

....

....

....

....

....

....

....

....

....

....

Fear

American poet Ralph Waldo Emerson said, "Always do what you are afraid to do."

Some decisions in life you know are momentous when you make them; other junctures only become apparent in hindsight. Sometimes we are at a crossroads and we don't even know it.

Mapping your past may help you find your future. Look back over the course of your life.

What turning points made all the difference? Where were the crossroads? Decision points?

=====

....

....

....

....

....

....

....

....

....

....

....

....

....

....

....

Draw your life as a series of routes, from one point to the next, with alternate junctures you could have taken, roads that led nowhere and had to be backtracked, and winding paths that brought you to a destination.

═══════════════

Were you ever lost (physically or spiritually)? What happened?

Looking back, list the decisions you made that changed the direction of your life for better or for worse.

===========

....

....

....

....

....

....

....

....

....

....

....

....

....

....

What choices do you face today that could impact the direction of your life?

....

....

....

....

....

....

....

....

....

....

....

....

....

....

....

Connecting Your Dreams and Goals

Some of us remember our dreams; others do not. You certainly can't control them. But can you learn from them? What might your dream life be trying to tell you? Can you go to sleep with a dream, and wake up with a purpose?

Date:

What was the dream about?

....

....

....

....

....

What action(s) is your dream
telling you to take?

....

....

....

....

....

....

....

....

....

....

Date:

What was the dream about?

....

....

....

....

....

What action(s) is your dream
telling you to take?

....

....

....

....

....

....

....

....

....

....

Date:
What was the dream about?

....

....

....

....

....

What action(s) is your dream telling you to take?

....

....

....

....

....

....

....

....

....

....

Date:
What was the dream about?

....
....
....
....
....

What action(s) is your dream
telling you to take?

....
....
....
....
....
....
....
....
....

Date:
What was the dream about?

....
....
....
....
....

What action(s) is your dream
telling you to take?

....
....
....
....
....
....
....
....
....
....

Date:
What was the dream about?

....

....

....

....

....

What action(s) is your dream
telling you to take?

....

....

....

....

....

....

....

....

....

....

Date:

What was the dream about?

....

....

....

....

....

What action(s) is your dream
telling you to take?

....

....

....

....

....

....

....

....

....

....

Date:

What was the dream about?

....

....

....

....

....

What action(s) is your dream
telling you to take?

....

....

....

....

....

....

....

....

....

....

Date:
What was the dream about?

....

....

....

....

....

What action(s) is your dream
telling you to take?

....

....

....

....

....

....

....

....

....

....

....

Date:

What was the dream about?

....
....
....
....
....

What action(s) is your dream
telling you to take?

....
....
....
....
....
....
....
....
....

Date:

What was the dream about?

....

....

....

....

....

What action(s) is your dream
telling you to take?

....

....

....

....

....

....

....

....

....

Date:

What was the dream about?

....

....

....

....

....

What action(s) is your dream
telling you to take?

....

....

....

....

....

....

....

....

....

....

Date:
What was the dream about?

....

....

....

....

....

What action(s) is your dream
telling you to take?

....

....

....

....

....

....

....

....

....

....

Date:

What was the dream about?

....

....

....

....

....

What action(s) is your dream
telling you to take?

....

....

....

....

....

....

....

....

....

....

Date:

What was the dream about?

....

....

....

....

....

What action(s) is your dream
telling you to take?

....

....

....

....

....

....

....

....

....

Date:

What was the dream about?

....

....

....

....

....

What action(s) is your dream
telling you to take?

....

....

....

....

....

....

....

....

....

....

Date:

What was the dream about?

....

....

....

....

....

What action(s) is your dream
telling you to take?

....

....

....

....

....

....

....

....

....

....

Dreams, Hunches, and Intuition

What do you daydream about?

....
....
....
....
....
....
....
....
....
....
....
....
....
....
....
....
....
....

Now try to daydream deliberately. Picture yourself living somewhere else. What does it look like? What are you doing?

....
....
....
....
....
....
....
....
....
....
....
....
....
....
....
....

What are your daydreams, hunches, and intuition telling you about yourself? What changes should you make?

....
....
....
....
....
....
....
....
....
....
....
....
....
....
....

What next? Now that you've committed to moving outside your comfort zone, how can you reinvigorate your life? First, determine the changes you want to make and the reasons you want to make them.

—————

"The journey of a thousand miles begins with a single step." —Lao Tzu

—————

Change I want to make:

....

....

....

Reason I want to make it:

....

....

....

....

Change I want to make:

....

....

....

....

Reason I want to make it:

....

....

....

Change I want to make:

....

....

....

....

Reason I want to make it:

....

....

....

....

Change I want to make:

....

....

....

....

Reason I want to make it:

....

....

....

Change I want to make:

....

....

....

....

Reason I want to make it:

....

....

....

....

Change I want to make:

....

....

....

....

Reason I want to make it:

....

....

....

Change I want to make:

....

....

....

....

Reason I want to make it:

....

....

....

Jim Davidson is among either the luckiest—or the unluckiest—men in the world. In his book, *The Ledge,* extreme climber Davidson writes about surviving a fall that killed his best friend, a friend who was tethered to him at the time. They had just summited Mount Rainier and were climbing down the opposite side, within sight of a ranger station. The snow gave way, plunging them to the bottom of an eighty-foot crevice inside the glacier. Mike Price was killed in the fall. Jim somehow found the will, and the ability, to rescue himself by climbing out of the glacier. Years later, Davidson was climbing Mount Everest when the Nepal earthquake wiped out the base camp below him. Two avalanches surrounded him. Aftershocks rumbled until they were rescued by helicopter.

Jim Davidson's resilience after the catastrophic death of his friend propelled him to continue. He climbed out of a glacier and kept climbing, all the way to Everest, where he got knocked down again.

Now "getting out of your 'zone' isn't always climbing to the top of Mount Everest—it's small changes, different choices that can allow you to be grateful and happy once you record and acknowledge that you are doing them," he writes.

Davidson's ascent of Everest—and he never did make it to the top, not yet anyway—began years earlier with tiny choices and small bouts of training. Whatever the changes we seek to make, the formula is the same.

What small changes could you make today that would change your tomorrow?

========

....

....

....

....

....

....

....

....

....

....

....

....

....

....

....

....

Tenacity

Mary Fasano always wished she had finished high school.
So after her husband died, she went back to school, and in 1979,
at the age of 71, earned her diploma. Mrs. Fasano did not stop
there. The Braintree, Massachusetts, mother of five began taking
the train into Cambridge to take courses at Harvard University.
In May 1997, she became the oldest person to earn a BA from the
Ivy League university. She was 89 years old.

Who is the most tenacious person you know? Why?

....

....

....

....

....

....

....

....

....

What one seemingly impossible thing would you like to accomplish?

How can your tenacious
role model inspire you?

....
....
....
....
....
....
....
....
....
....
....
....
....
....
....
....

Make Your Own Luck

Molly Goldberg was Amnesty International's campus representative at her community college in Colorado. She implemented many innovative ideas at her college chapter but was frustrated by the limits of what she could accomplish. Molly decided that what the organization needed was new blood on the board of directors, younger blood—in fact, her blood. She launched a write-in campaign to be added to the ballot and was elected. Molly made her own luck.

Does success come from hard work, luck, or a combination of both?

....
....
....
....
....
....
....
....
....
....
....
....
....
....
....
....
....
....

Old Habits Die Hard

So we've agreed it's time to shake things up. What's next?

The most effective change is incremental, habitual. In the past decade there's been much study about habit—why we have habits and how to change them. The science is clear: setting small goals, following through on a daily basis, and recording and measuring your results can lead to sustained change.

Incremental progress, and the celebration of intermediate success, is the key to lasting change.

How do you change your trajectory in life after you've launched?

....

....

....

....

....

....

....

....

What "midcourse corrections" might benefit your own life?

===============

....

....

....

....

....

....

....

....

....

....

....

....

....

....

People fear change for all sorts of reasons. Some of us are naturally novelty averse (neophobes). Others seek out sensation at every turn, embracing the new (neophiles). These natural tendencies drive our ability and willingness to shake things up and change what we've been doing. Are you a neophile or a neophobe?

━━━━━━━━━

Describe new things you have tried or places you have gone that excited you.

New thing I tried:

....

....

How did it make me feel?

....

....

....

New thing I tried:

....

....

....

....

How did it make me feel?

....

....

....

....

New thing I tried:

....

....

....

....

How did it make me feel?

....

....

....

....

Describe a time you avoided trying something new because you were scared.

....

....

....

....

....

....

....

....

....

....

....

....

....

....

Describe a time you tried something new even though you were terrified.

....

....

....

....

....

....

....

....

....

....

....

....

....

....

Going to new places or meeting new
people can jump-start your brain.
Our brains are wired to remember new
things more clearly than familiar or
habitual ones. There is no better way
to reignite your life than by trying
something new, just as there is no
better way to overcome fear than by
doing what frightens us.

A new experience I want to try:

....

....

....

Why?

....

....

....

A new experience I want to try:

....

....

....

....

Why?

....

....

....

....

A new experience I want to try:

....

....

....

....

Why?

....

....

....

....

Renew:
Timing Is Everything

It may seem that there are not enough hours in the day, but when it comes to change, a clock, a calendar, and a timer are your friends. First, let's look at how you spend your time.

Of all the things you do daily, what are a few things you would happily never do again?

....

....

....

....

....

....

....

....

....

What changes can you make to eliminate these things from your life?

....

....

....

....

....

....

....

....

....

....

....

....

....

....

If you were given an extra hour a day, how would you spend it?

....

....

....

....

....

....

....

....

....

....

....

....

....

....

....

Allow Room to Grow

Avant-garde musician Sun Ra titled his 1974 film *Space Is the Place*. Though his wandering astro-narrative clearly references outer space (Sun Ra claimed to hail from a planet other than Earth), he was right in this regard: when it comes to how you feel, space is indeed the place. Our surroundings influence us in subtle but significant ways. Controlling your environment can be the key to controlling your outlook.

What kind of secret place did you have as a child? Describe it.

....

....

....

....

....

....

....

....

....

What spaces inspire you?

....

....

....

....

....

....

....

....

....

....

....

....

....

....

....

What spaces inspire you?
(continued)

....

....

....

....

....

....

....

....

....

....

....

....

....

....

....

....

What spaces inspire you?
(continued)

....
....
....
....
....
....
....
....
....
....
....
....
....
....
....
....

What did you like about the hottest place you've ever been? The coldest?

....
....
....
....
....
....

What's the loudest place you've ever been? The quietest?

....
....
....
....
....
....

If you could add one feature to your home or office space, what would it be? What would you do there?

....
....
....
....
....
....
....
....
....
....
....
....
....
....

Simplify

Sometimes we need to make space for new things. Embracing simplicity can alleviate stress and create energy for new, different choices. Reducing the clutter around us promotes peace and vitality. Try it now. Clear out a small drawer or a section of your closet.

How did deciding to discard things make you feel? Lighter? Anxious?

....

....

....

....

....

....

....

....

....

....

Decide to discard one additional thing each day even if it's just an old magazine. Make a plan to make some space in your life for what's next.

================

....

....

....

....

....

....

....

....

....

....

....

....

....

Connect

Just as the space around us impacts our inner life and motivation, so do the people with whom we interact. Spend time with people who want to spend time with you. Hang out with folks whose company you enjoy. Seek out people who make you feel like a better version of yourself. Find people with the qualities you admire. Be around people who spend their time doing worthwhile things. Negativity and toxicity are contagious. Sure, we all need to vent a little here and there. We all have legitimate reasons to complain, and we need people in our lives that love us and will listen. But seeking out happy, positive people will make you a happier, more positive person. That doesn't mean you have to jettison the whiners completely. Just notice what's going on around you and adjust as needed.

List the people you spend the most time with and why you enjoy them.

....
....
....
....
....
....
....
....
....
....
....
....
....
....
....

Is it possible to adjust your life so you are spending your days with those who enrich your life and have your back?

So, What Have

You've learned that you are okay just the way you are. This journal may have helped reinvigorate your resolve or your experience, but fundamentally, you're doing just fine without it.

═══════════════

You've learned to identify and lead from your strengths, because you can't lead from the broken places. You are stronger than you knew.

═══════════════

You've learned that adding is more fun than subtracting, that models of deprivation don't work, and that the world is filled with an abundance of wonderful things, enough for everybody.

═══════════════

You've learned that things will work out—they always do. It might not be the outcome you thought it would be, but in the end it will be okay.

═══════════════

You've learned to find the fun. There is whimsy and humor and delight to be had every day, but you have to make room for it.

You Learned?

You've learned to see the good and keep your eyes on all that's good and beautiful and possible. The world is filled with wonderful things just waiting to be noticed.

═══════════

And most important, you've learned that the stories you tell create the person you become. Telling your story in a different way can reshape your life without changing one thing about it.

═══════════

Remember, what gets measured gets done. Continue to track your progress in areas of your life that are important to you. It's the most effective way to stay on course and get outside your comfort zone!

THESE SEVEN THINGS WE KNOW TO BE TRUE:

1. You're okay just as you are.
2. Lead with your strengths.
3. Adding is more fun than subtracting.
4. Things will work out—they always do.
5. Find the fun.
6. See the good.
7. The stories we tell create the people we become.

Quarto is the authority on a wide range of topics.

Quarto educates, entertains and enriches the lives of
our readers—enthusiasts and lovers of hands-on living.

www.quartoknows.com

First published in the United States of America in 2016 by
Rock Point , a member of
Quarto Publishing Group USA Inc.
142 West 36th Street, 4th Floor
New York, NY 10018
quartoknows.com

10 9 8 7 6 5 4 3 2 1

ISBN: 978-1-63106-265-0

Coloring pages © Fishscraps, Carrie Stephens
Design by Leah Lococo

Printed in China

MIX
Paper from
responsible sources
FSC® C016973